Abraham Lincoln

Abe had one older sister, Sarah, and a younger brother who died at the age of two.

The Man Who Held a Nation Together!

On February 12, 1809, Abraham Lincoln was born in a tiny log cabin on a small farm in Kentucky. When he was seven, his family was forced to leave their farm. His father, Thomas Lincoln, decided to move the family to the wilderness of Indiana.

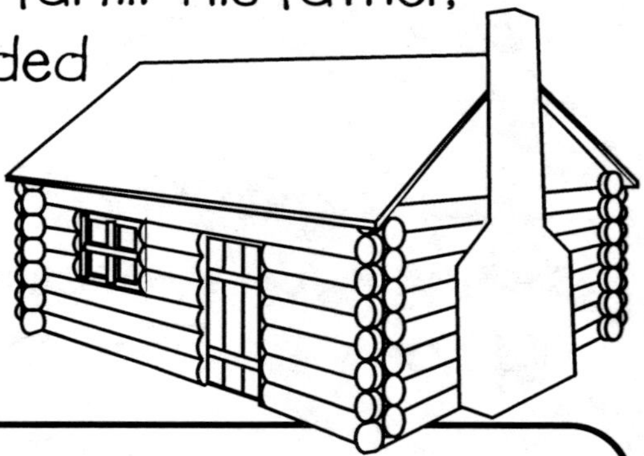

Color the log cabin.

Find out what the Lincolns had to cross by holding this page up to a mirror. Write the answer below.

Ohio River

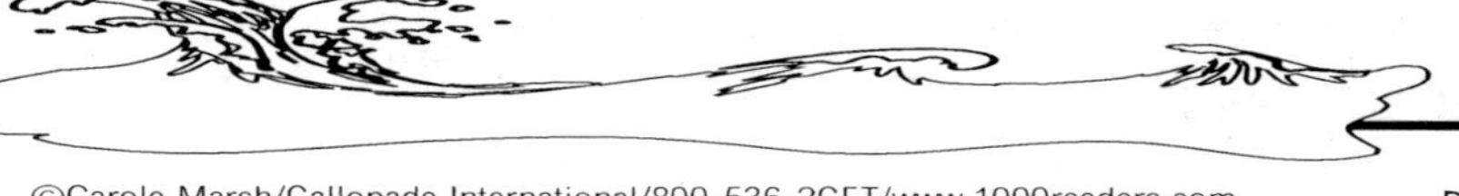

©Carole Marsh/Gallopade International/800-536-2GET/www.1000readers.com
This page is not reproducible.

Abe was tall for his age and a hard worker. He worked outside from dawn to dark and was skilled at using an axe. He was so good at splitting rails that he was later nicknamed "the Rail-Splitter." The Lincolns were poor and Abe had to work so much to earn a living that he rarely had the chance to go to school.

Color the axe and log.

Abe's mother died in 1819 from milk sickness. Solve the problem to learn how old Abe was when she died.

```
  1819 (year mother died)
- 1809 (year Abe was born)
       (age at mother's death)
```

When Abe did go to school, he had to walk 2 miles each way! He thought of school as a real treat.

A year after Abe's mother died, his father married Sarah Bush Johnston, a widow with three children. Sarah brought love and warmth to the Lincoln family. She nurtured Abraham's love of reading and encouraged him to better himself. He called her his "best friend in the world."

Abe had a special name for his stepmother. Starting with U, cross off every other letter to find out this special name.

U A H N C G R E K L N M T O J T K H Q E L R

_____   _____

There were few books on the frontier—Abe walked many miles to borrow all he could. His family owned one book—the Bible.

The Lincolns moved to Illinois when Abe was 21. He worked as a deckhand, store clerk, woodcutter, and soldier. He then ran his own store. One day, he bought a large barrel full of odds and ends. In it, he found a famous law book. After studying it night after night, he decided to become a lawyer.

Abe grew to be 6 feet, 4 inches tall! How tall is this in inches only?

Abe was _____ inches tall.

(HINT: 12 inches = 1 foot)

Abe was tall, thin, awkward, and not good-looking. His rough black hair stood up on his head!

In 1834, Abe was elected to the Illinois House of Representatives. Three years later, he joined a law office in Springfield. His boss introduced him to Mary Todd, a quick-tempered, educated young woman. Abe fell in love with her and they were married in 1842.

Color the wedding bells.

Lincoln became widely known as a good and honest lawyer. His nickname became: (circle the answer)

Honest Abe

Pioneer Abe

Preacher Abe

Mary often nagged Abe about his lack of education. She called him "common." He just smiled and agreed!

Page 5

Abe soon became more involved in government. However, this road was not easy for him. He would win an election, then lose one. In all, he lost 5 times, but he won 6 times—the sixth one being as president of the United States!

Color the vote button.

Find the words in the Word Find.

LINCOLN   DEBATE   LAWYER

Not many people knew of Abe until his famous debate with Stephen Douglas, a supporter of slavery.

L	D	E	B
A	C	I	S
W	T	S	E
Y	L	G	M
E	B	F	I
R	K	L	P
D	L	I	N
I	B	L	O

Abe and Mary had four sons—Robert, Eddie, Willie, and Tad. Eddie died when he was only 4 years old.

Abe was a loving father who enjoyed spending time with his sons. His loved to sit in his favorite chair, with his boys romping on the floor around his long legs. His pet name for the boys was "dear little codgers."

ILLINOIS   HONEST   TALL

A   T   E   S
K   F   I   J
N   O   H   N
N   O   R   C
J   Q   E   T
D   G   M   H
C   O   L   N
L   L   A   T

Lincoln had a gift for telling stories. He could always make people laugh.

Lincoln lost his son Willie to a fever in 1862. He was full of grief because he was very close to Willie.

Lincoln entered the presidency with a major problem—the southern states were seceding from the Union. Six weeks after coming into office, Lincoln declared war on the southern states when the Confederates fired on the Union-held Fort Sumter in Charleston, South Carolina.

Many southerners were upset Lincoln had been elected president because he was against slavery.

Lincoln had problems with the Union generals and tried one after another before he found a good one. Who was it? Solve the code to find out!

U L Y S S E S

S   G R A N T

Lincoln said, "the moment came when I felt that slavery must die that the nation might live." On September 22, 1862, he issued the Emancipation Proclamation. This outlawed slavery in all southern states. Although the nation was at war and he had no power to enforce it, it was a major step in the anti-slavery movement.

> Lincoln realized the Constitution would have to be amended to end slavery. He began working on such an amendment.

Complete the math problem to find out what amendment that later ended slavery in the United States

$3 + 7 - 5 + 10 + 3 - 8 + 10 + 9 - 7 + 5 - 7 - 4 - 3$

It was the _____ th Amendment.

When the Civil War ended in 1865, Lincoln stated that he wanted to restore the Union peacefully and quickly. Four days later, he was shot while at the theater. He died the next morning on April 15. The nation mourned this terrific president from humble beginnings, who withstood terrible stress and heartache to hold the nation together.

John Wilkes Booth, a southern sympathizer, shot Lincoln.

Color the picture.

By preserving the Union, Lincoln influenced the course of world history.

Lincoln lost his son Tad to sickness during the war.

Glossary

amendment: a change in, or addition to, a constitution, law, or bill

codger: an odd or strange fellow

emancipation: set free from slavery or strict control

humble: modest or meek

proclamation: an official public statement

sympathizer: one who shares the feelings or ideas of another person or group

Pop Quiz!

1. Being handy with an axe, Abe was often called:
   ○ Axe Man
   ○ Rail-Splitter
   ○ Paul Bunyan

2. Abe had many jobs before he decided to be a:
   ○ teacher
   ○ minister
   ○ lawyer

3. Abe was not well-educated, rich or:
   ○ handsome
   ○ tall
   ○ funny

4. Abe was president during the bloody:
   ○ Civil War
   ○ American Revolution
   ○ World War I

5. Abe's speech that was a step towards ending slavery was the:
   ○ Gettysburg Address
   ○ Emancipation Proclamation
   ○ Declaration of Independence